CHRONICLES OF THE CURSED SWORD

Volume 15

Story by
YEO BEOP-RYONG
Art by
PARK HUI-JIN

HAMBURG // LONDON // LOS ANGELES // TOKYO

Chronicles of the Cursed Sword Vol. 15

Written by Yeo Beop-Ryong

Illustrated by Park Hui-Jin

Translation - Youngju Ryu
English Adaptation - Matt Varosky
Copy Editor - Hope Donovan
Retouch and Lettering - Jason Milligan
Production Artist - Mike Estacio
Cover Design - Kyle Plummer

Editor - Aaron Suhr
Digital Imaging Manager - Chris Buford
Managing Editor - Lindsey Johnston
VP of Production - Ron Klamert
Publisher - Mike Kiley
Editor-In-Chief - Rob Tokar
President and C.O.O. - John Parker
C.E.O. and Chief Creative Officer - Stuart Levy

A  Manga

TOKYOPOP Inc.
5900 Wilshire Blvd. Suite 2000
Los Angeles, CA 90036

E-mail: info@TOKYOPOP.com
Come visit us online at www.TOKYOPOP.com

ISBN: 1-59532-647-2

First TOKYOPOP printing: May 2006

10 9 8 7 6 5 4 3 2 1

Printed in the USA

Chronicles

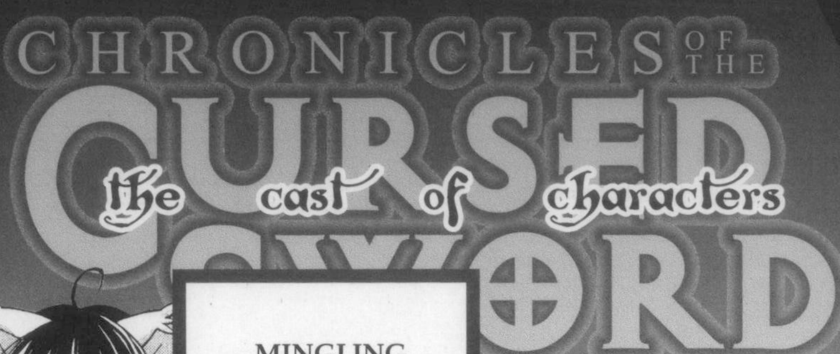

MINGLING

A lesser demon with feline qualities, Mingling is now the loyal follower of Shyao Lin. She lives in fear of Rey, who still doesn't trust her.

THE PASA SWORD

A living sword that hungers for demon blood. It grants its user incredible power, but at a great cost—it can take over the user's body and, in time, his soul.

JARYOON
KING OF HAHYUN

Noble and charismatic, Jaryoon is the stuff of which great kings are made. But there has been a drastic change in Jaryoon as of late. Now under the sway of the spirit of the PaChun sword, Jaryoon is cutting a swath of humanity across the countryside as he searches for his new prey: Rey.

SHYAO LIN

A sorceress, previously Rey's traveling companion and greatest ally. Shyao has recently discovered that she is, in fact, one of the Eight Sages of the Azure Pavilion, sent to gather information in the Human Realm. Much to her dismay, she has been told that she must now kill Rey Yan.

REY YAN

Rey has proven to be a worthy student of the wise and diminutive Master Chen Kaihu. At the Mujin Fortress, the ultimate warrior testing grounds, Rey has shown his martial arts mettle. And with both the possessed Jaryoon and the now godlike Shyao after his blood—he'll need all the survival skills he can muster.

MOOSUNGJE
EMPEROR OF ZHOU
Until recently, the kingdom of Zhou under Moosungje's reign was a peaceful place, its people prosperous, its foreign relations amicable. But recently, Moosungje has undergone a mysterious change, leading Zhou to war against its neighbors.
SORCERESS OF THE UNDERWORLD
A powerful sorceress, she was approached by Shiyan's agents to team up with the Demon Realm. For now, her motives are unclear, but she's not to be trusted...
SHIYAN
PRIME MINISTER OF HAHYUN
A powerful sorcerer who is in league with the Demon Realm and plots to take over the kingdom. He is the creator of the PaSa Sword and its match, the PaChun Sword—the Cursed Swords that may be the keys to victory.
CHEN KAIHU
A diminutive martial arts master. In Rey, he sees a promising pupil—one who can learn his powerful techniques.

Thus Far In...

CHRONICLES OF THE CURSED SWORD

In an era of warring states, warlords become kings, dynasties crumble, and heroes can rise from the most unlikely places. Rey Yan was an orphan with no home, no skills and no purpose. But when he comes upon the PaSa sword, a cursed blade made from the bones of the Demon Emperor, he suddenly finds himself with the power to be a great hero...

In his efforts to turn back the demon invasion of the human realm, Rey fights a desperate battle against the Sorcerer King, with the life of Hyacia at stake! Just as all hope seems lost, Rey is contacted by Renshou, the soul whose body Hyacia now inhabits. With Renshou's help, they defeat the Sorcerer King, free Hyacia and continue their journey toward the Great Azure Pavilion. Meanwhile, King Jaryoon, still under the influence of the PaChun Sword, has become increasingly merciless as he makes his way homeward...

Chapter 59:
Explosion

THE SOLDIERS' ENDURANCE IS WANING, SHIYAN.
HOW LONG DO YOU THINK THEY WILL LAST?
A MONTH AT MOST, KING JARYOON.
HOW LONG UNTIL THE EXPEDITIONARY FORCE IS ASSEMBLED? WE CAN'T START THE CAMPAIGN UNTIL THEY ARE READY.
A FORTNIGHT... IF WE ARE LUCKY.
HOWEVER, THEIR COMMANDER HAS ALREADY BEEN CREATED. WOULD MY LORD LIKE TO SEE HIM?
WAS HIS MIND ABLE TO SURVIVE YOUR MANIPULATIONS? I HOPE YOU LEFT HIM MORE THAN JUST A BLANK PAGE.
HIS MENTAL CAPACITY IS ABOUT THE SAME AS WHEN HE WAS A LIVING BEING.

HIS LOYALTY TO YOUR MAJESTY HAS BEEN MAGNIFIED...

...BUT I DIDN'T REALLY CHANGE HIM IN OTHER REGARDS.

GOOD.

WE'LL STRIKE THE GREAT AZURE PAVILION BEFORE THE MONTH IS UP.

MAKE SURE EVERYTHING IS READY.

WHAT IS HAPPENING ?!
INCREDIBLE!

LIGHTNING FLASHES AND AN EARTH-QUAKE...
SOME-THING HAS HAPPENED.
THE FLASHES COME FROM THE DIRECTION OF THE CAPITAL!
IT IS THE POWER OF THE DIVINE REALM MANIFESTED HERE ON EARTH.
WHAT ARE THOSE GODS UP TO NOW?

RUIN SUCH AS THIS ACCOMPANIES A DEITY'S SELF-DESTRUCTION.
HMPH.
I AM REMINDED OF WHEN THE WARRIOR LORD OF THE DIVINE REALM DESTROYED HIMSELF 500 YEARS AGO.
THE ONLY DIFFERENCE NOW WOULD BE THAT IT IS HAPPENING IN THE HUMAN REALM.
COULD THIS BE THE BEGINNING OF WHAT I FEAR?

ARE THEY
REALLY GOING TO
DESTROY EVERY
LIVING THING IN THE
HUMAN REALM?

!!
WE HAVE TO
FIND OUT.

!

WE MUST
GO TO THE
CAPITAL.

IF THEY HAVE HURT MY BROTHER THE EMPEROR IN ANY WAY... I'LL SKIN EVERY LAST ONE OF THEM ALIVE!

HEH HEH.

JARYOON'S SPEED IS MARVELOUS. HIS POWER HAS BECOME INCREDIBLE.

NOW, IF HE CAN ABSORB THE POWER OF THE HEAVENLY SAGES WITH THE PACHUN SWORD, EVERYTHING WILL BE READY.

THE PROBLEM IS, WHERE DO WE FIND SAGES IN THE HUMAN REALM?

!

WHAT TOOK PLACE HERE?
I...I CAN'T BELIEVE WHAT I'M SEEING.

THE IMPERIAL CAPITAL...IT'S JUST GONE!
WITH THE DESTRUCTION SO COMPLETE, JARYOON, I'M AFRAID THERE CAN BE NO SURVIVORS.
WHERE ARE THE PEOPLE... WHERE IS HIS MAJESTY, MY BROTHER?
YOU ASS!

YOU TOLD ME THAT MY BROTHER WOULD BE FINE-- THAT HE'D COME TO NO HARM!
I DID SAY THAT, DIDN'T I?
BUT TO BE CLEAR, I WAS ONLY TALKING ABOUT THE THREAT FROM THE DEMON RACE, THAT THEY WOULD WANT HIM AS A HOSTAGE, AND THAT HE'D BE USEFUL TO THEM ONLY IF HE WAS ALIVE.
BUT THIS IS NOT THE DEMONS' DOING. DEITIES OF THE HEAVENLY REALM HAVE DONE THIS, HAVE STARTED THIS WAR, WITHOUT CARING WHAT WILL HAPPEN TO THE HUMAN RACE.
THIS KIND OF DESTRUCTION CAN ONLY HAVE ONE CAUSE. A DREADNOUGHT, A WARRIOR DEITY CLAD IN FULL HEAVENLY ARMOR, HAS DESTROYED HIMSELF.
THIS SAME KIND OF DESTRUCTION BURNED UP THE ENTIRE DEMON REALM FIVE HUNDRED YEARS AGO. AND NOW IT'S BEING USED IN THE HUMAN REALM.

I WILL KILL THEM ALL, SHIYAN...

WHEN I'M DONE WITH THEM...

...THERE WILL BE NOTHING LEFT OF THE HEAVENLY REALM!

THE ONES LEFT ON THAT SHIP, FOR EXAMPLE.

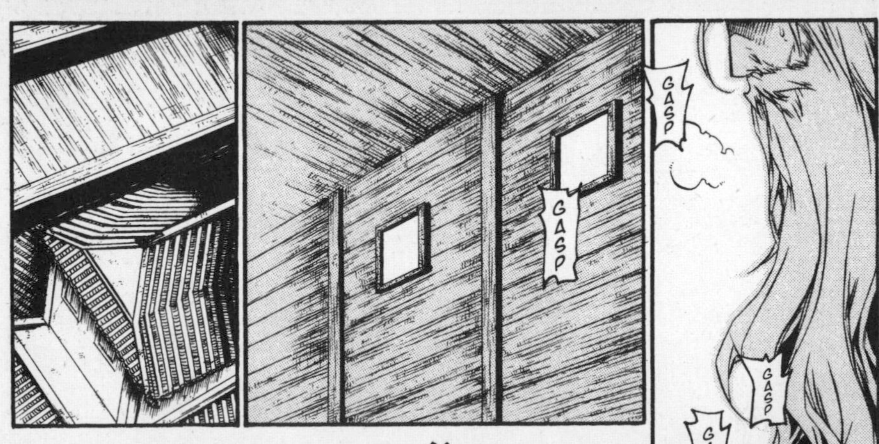

GASP
GASP
GASP
I HAVE TO GET OUT OF HERE AND FIND HELP FOR HER...
비틀...
A SOUND...
YOU THERE! COME NOT ANY CLOSER!

A MAN?
HOW CAN A MERE MAN EMIT SUCH DEMONIC ENERGY?
...
WHO ARE YOU?
I AM JARYOON, THE KING OF HAHYUN.
YOU HAVE REDUCED MY LAND TO ASHES!
KING OF HAHYUN
YES, WE SAGES ARE PARTLY TO BLAME FOR THE PRESENT STATE OF AFFAIRS.
BUT ALL THIS... IS TO PREVENT THE DEMON EMPEROR FROM REEMERGING.
!!
SHUT UP!

BECAUSE OF YOU, MY BROTHER IS LOST!
IT MAKES NO DIFFERENCE TO ME WHY YOU DID WHAT YOU DID!
AND YOU'LL PAY FOR THAT... WITH YOUR LIFE!

HAH.
I DON'T KNOW WHAT KIND BLACK MAGIC YOU PRACTICE, BUT DO YOU REALLY THINK YOU CAN HARM ME? I AM LORD HEIAN, LEADER OF THE EIGHT GREAT SAGES OF THE AZURE PAVILION!

GRRR...

YOU THINK YOU CAN BLOCK THE PACHUN SWORD WITH THAT?

THE PACHUN SWORD ?!

DEMONS OF THE EIGHT FIERY HELLS, I COMMAND YOU TO SHOW YOURSELVES!

수와
THIS IS...THE POWER OF THE DEMON REALM!
HOW CAN A MERE HUMAN BEING COMMAND IT?
퇴아아아아아아아아...
GAH!

KEEP AWAY FROM ME, DEMONS!
HUCK
HUCK

Lightning of Hell!

RANA...
DEAR RANA...

I THOUGHT A SAGE WOULD PROVIDE GREATER POWER FOR THE PACHUN SWORD...
I GUESS I'LL HAVE TO GO FIND MORE OF THEM.
NOW...
SHALL WE TAKE A LOOK AT WHAT THE OLD MAN WAS TRYING SO HARD TO PROTECT?

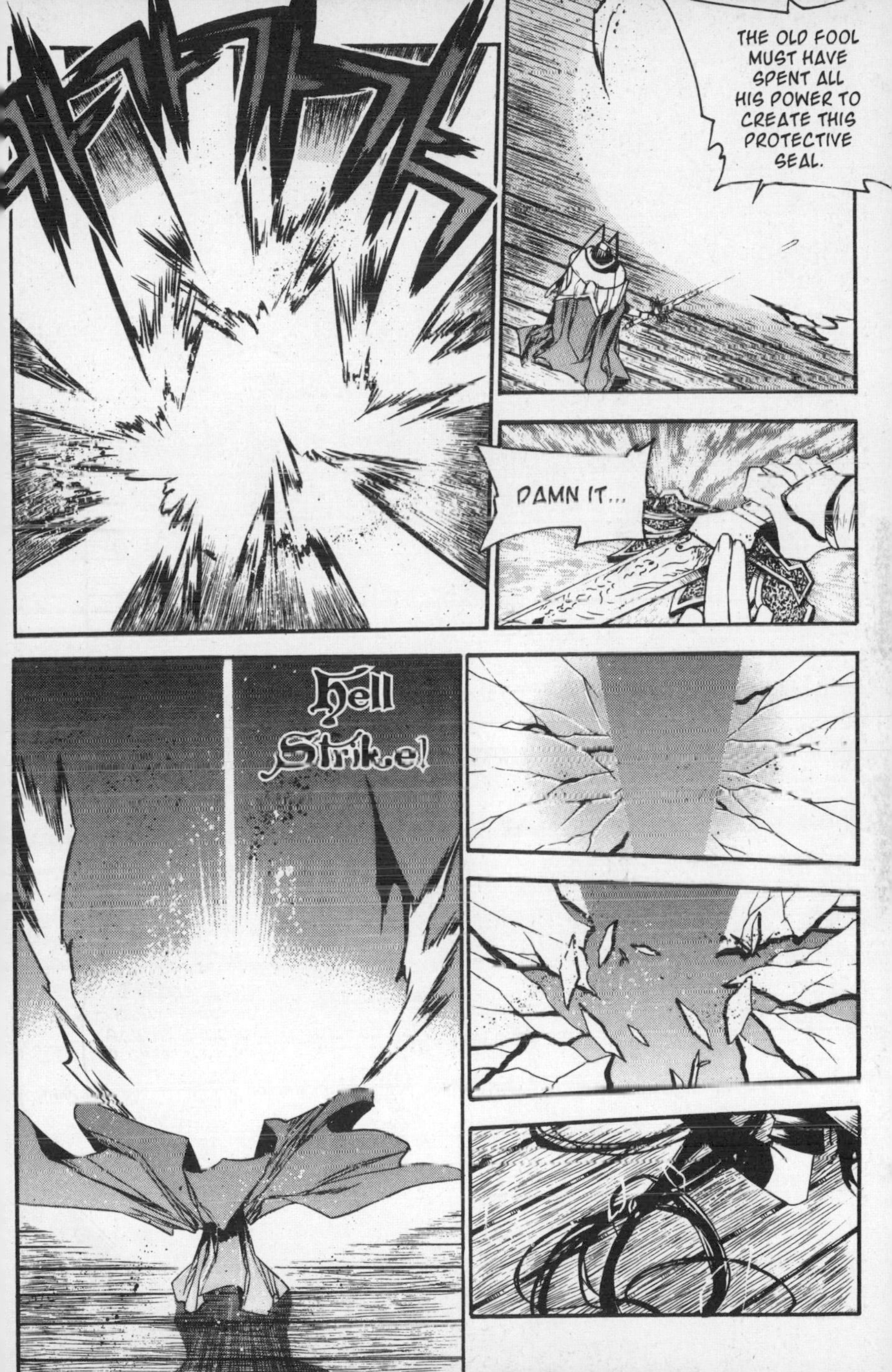
THE OLD FOOL MUST HAVE SPENT ALL HIS POWER TO CREATE THIS PROTECTIVE SEAL.
DAMN IT...
Hell Strike!

......
아...
S... SHYAO?!
WHAT...WHAT IS SHE DOING HERE?!

SHE EMANATES REMARKABLY POWERFUL AND PURE ENERGY, EVEN FOR A SAGE.

ARE YOU GOING TO SLAY HER AND LET THE PACHUN SWORD ABSORB THAT ENERGY?

NO... NEVER! NOT IN A MILLION YEARS!

SHE'S INJURED...

WE'RE TAKING HER BACK TO THE CAMP, **NOW!**

JARYOON HAS KILLED THE GIRL'S GRANDFATHER, NOT KNOWING THAT SHE IS REALLY THE LADY SOHWA, ONE OF THE EIGHT GREAT SAGES!

—.

HMM...

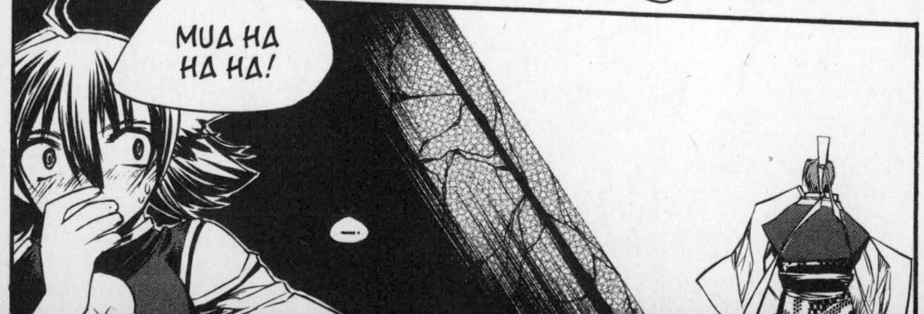

Chapter 60:
To the Great
Azure Pavilion

저벅
저벅
AHH...
AH-CHOO!
A COLD?
LOUEN, COVER YOUR MOUTH. REY, WHERE TO NOW?
WE CONTINUE ON TO THE GREAT AZURE PAVILION, LIKE WE PLANNED.
HOPEFULLY IT WON'T BE MUCH FARTHER, RIGHT MINXIA?
RIGHT. WE JUST HAVE TO PASS OUT OF THE POWER FIELD PUT OFF BY THE SORCERERS' FORTRESS.

THIS IS IT!

MINXIA, WHERE DOES THIS LEAD?

COME ON, EVERYBODY, LET'S GO!
WHOAAAA!!
?!

YIKES!
UGH!
I'M GONNA THROW UP!
...
WHA?
THIS... LOOKS LIKE JUST AN ORDINARY HOUSE.

...EH?
UGH!
OWWW!
HEY...
THAT'S STRANGE.
THIS IS THE INN, BUT THERE'S NOBODY HERE. I SENT THEM A MESSAGE TO HAVE SOMEONE GREET US.
GROAN!
YIKES.
COUGH!
COUGH!
OWWW.

OH, HELLO! LADY MINXIA, WELCOME!
HEY, YOU'RE LATE! YOU SHOULD'VE BEEN HERE TO MEET US!
HMPH!
I'M SO SORRY. IT WAS BECAUSE OF THE SUDDEN EARTHQUAKE ...
EVERY-THING IS A MESS. BUT THANKFULLY, BECAUSE OF THE PROTECTIVE SPELL, WE DIDN'T SUFFER TOO MUCH DAMAGE.
!!

STILL, THIS LOOKS WORSE THAN THE LAST BIG EARTHQUAKE YEARS AGO.

YOU SHOULD WAIT UNTIL YOU GO OUTSIDE.

WAIT UNTIL YOU SEE THE DAMAGE OUT THERE.

PSST, MAO! IF THIS IS THE SOUTHERN PREFECTURE...
I KNOW, THEN IT MEANS WE'RE CLOSE TO THE GREAT AZURE PAVILION!
THIS EARTHQUAKE, IT DOESN'T LOOK LIKE IT OCCURRED NATURALLY.
SO, YOU GUYS ARE IMPRESSED?
아하하하하
WHAT YOU'RE SEEING WAS ONE OF THE SORCERERS' TOOLS FOR CONTROLLING THE HUMAN REALM BEFORE REY DEFEATED THEM.
THERE ARE SEVERAL SECRET PORTALS LIKE THIS THAT LINK THE SORCERERS' FORTRESS DIRECTLY TO DIFFERENT PARTS OF THE HUMAN REALM!

TO THINK THAT A REGULAR OLD INN WAS A SECRET SORCERERS' BASE!

AMAZING!

HA HA! AND IT'S BEEN UNDER THE SAGES' NOSES FOR OVER 200 YEARS!

SIGH...
HOW-EVER...
THE SORCERERS' FORTRESS HAS NOW SUSTAINED SO MUCH DAMAGE THAT WE'LL PROBABLY HAVE TO CLOSE DOWN ALL OF OUR BASES HERE.
TIME TO SAY GOODBYE.
I MUST GO BACK NOW. UNTIL NEXT TIME, MEOW!
PHEW! THE SMELL OF THE DEAD IS AWFUL HERE!

AH!
BUT SO MANY CORPSES MEAN WE CAN GET YOU A NEW ARM, SHISHAN! JUST YOU WAIT, MY LITTLE CREATION!
DANGLE
DANGLE
YOU KIDS GO AHEAD. I'LL CATCH UP WITH YOU WHEN I'M DONE.
DR. LAOBI, WE CAN'T LET YOU DESECRATE THE DEAD LIKE THAT!
WHY NOT?
DO YOU WANT TO VOLUNTEER YOUR ARM, THEN?
HMM?
IT DOESN'T MATTER IF YOU THREATEN ME...
...I CAN'T LET YOU COMMIT AN ATROCITY!
GULP!
MAO!
...I CAN'T FORGIVE IT, NOT WHEN WE'RE SO CLOSE TO THE PAVILION...
GULP...
I...

...I WON'T...
...STAND FOR IT...
I'M GOING TO COUNT TO THREE.
ONE...
TWO...
NEXT TIME, I WILL DRAW BLOOD.
IN THE FUTURE I WON'T BE SO GENEROUS, LITTLE SAGE.
I PROMISE I WON'T DO ANYTHING!
AHHH! FORGIVE ME! I WON'T GET IN YOUR WAY AGAIN...
HEE HEE HEE!

NICE BACKBONE, LOUEN. WE'LL SEE YOU LATER, DR. LAOBI.
엉엉엉엉엉!
YOU COMING, REY?
BYE!

탁

탁

HELP!

?!

YOU'VE GOT TO HELP ME! PLEASE, A WOMAN IS TRAPPED IN THE RUBBLE.
WE NEED MANPOWER TO GET HER OUT! HELP US, PLEASE!
REALLY?!
LOUEN, LET'S GO HELP THEM!
HEY, BUT WHEN I ASK FOR HELP YOU LOOK AWAY?!
COME ON, DON'T BE PETTY.
LET'S GO.
I AM NOT PETTY!
QUICKLY, SHE'S IN HERE!

SOMETHING FELL FROM THE SKY AND ALL THE BUILDINGS COLLAPSED.
으앙
으앙
WE CAN STILL HEAR HER VOICE COMING FROM WITHIN.
OH, MY!
WE HAVE TO HURRY AND GET HER OUT!
—...

REY?

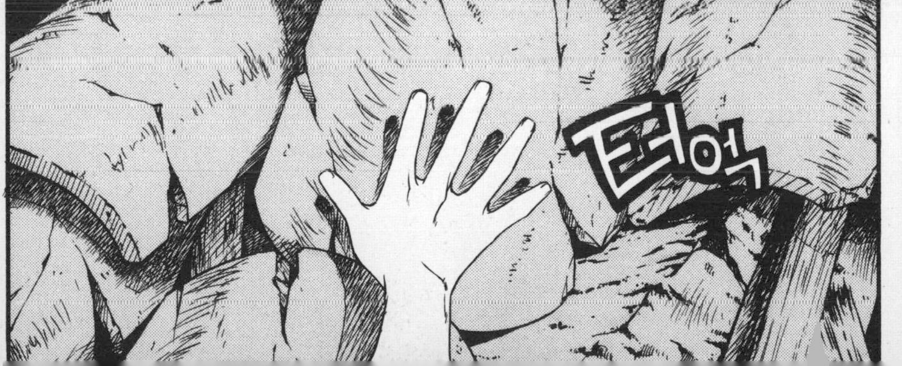

Element: metal!

쾅
쾅
쾅
쾅
쾅
WHAT INCREDIBLE STRENGTH! LIKE HE'S MADE OF STEEL! HE THROWS THOSE BOULDERS LIKE THEY'RE PEBBLES!

HELP ME...
!
UGH...
PASA SWORD!

YOW!
YOU NEARLY SLASHED MY FACE!
SHUT UP!
SOB
SOB

SOB...
SNIFFLE...
SNIFF
YOU NEARLY KILLED ME!
SNIFF
SNIFF
훌쩍
——...

A SAGE? I'VE NEVER BEEN SO INSULTED!

.....

DO I LOOK THAT DEVIOUS AND CRUEL?

YOU HURT MY FEELINGS...

IS THAT WOMAN CRYING OVER THERE?
웅성
웅성
REY, WHAT DID YOU DO TO HER? PEOPLE ARE STARING...
REY--?
SNIFF...
WAAAH...WAAAAAAAHHH!!!
HEY, COME ON NOW...
HEY...
LOOK, I'M SORRY... DON'T CRY...
BWAAAA!!
I SAID DON'T CRY!
울컥
울컥
C'MON, SERIOUSLY...
WOULD YOU STOP ALREADY?

오싹
IF I HAVE TO LISTEN TO THAT WHINY LITTLE NOISE YOU'RE MAKING FOR ONE MORE SECOND, I'LL KILL YOU!
....
히끅
히끅
SHUT. UP.
WHOA...
HE HEARD YOU, STUPID! RUN!
THAT GUY'S A JERK!
하아
...

I WONDER WHAT'S KEEPING DR. LAOBI? SHE LEFT US HERE ALL ALONE WITH REY.
SNIFF
I HOPE SHE WASN'T CAUGHT STEALING THE LIMBS OFF OF A CORPSE.
GIVES NEW MEANING TO "ARMED" ROBBERY.
LOUEN! MAO! PAY ATTENTION. WE NEED TO FIGURE OUT WHAT A DEMON IS DOING HERE.
하아
WHAT ?!
A DEMON? WHO?

SITTING RIGHT BEFORE YOUR EYES.
HER?!
BUT SHE DOESN'T EMIT DEMON ENERGY. IF ANYTHING, I'D SAY SHE IS A SAGE!
BESIDES, SOMEONE SO PRETTY CAN'T BE A DEMON!

I'M HERE...
I KNEW IT.
BUT WHAT ARE YOU DOING HERE?
AHA!
SORRY, BUT HE'S RIGHT. I AM A DEMON.
...BECAUSE THOSE CRUEL SAGES ATTACKED OUR HOUSE!
YOUR HOUSE?
!!!

Chapter 61:
Sages' Defeat

IT WAS A COUPLE DAYS AGO...

ACK...!

LINGTSE, WHAT ARE YOU DOING?!

PAORIN BOTHERS ME EVERY DAY, AND NOW YOU, TOO?

EH?

LINGTSE?

UP THERE...A FLYING SHIP IS APPROACHING US!

A SHIP?

OH, THAT? I KNOW WHAT THOSE ARE. THEY'RE THE SHIPS THAT THE HEAVENLY SAGES USE.

WAIT, **SAGES?!** THAT MEANS OUR **ENEMIES** ARE COMING, STUPID!

MASTER TAORUN!

BUT I DON'T WANT TO FIGHT...

HEE HEE!
I CAN'T WAIT TO MAKE MINCEMEAT OF THE SAGES, PAORIN!
GOOD. THE POPULATION OF THIS CITY IS ONLY 230,000, SO I CAN ONLY USE THE DEMON GATE SUMMONING SPELL ONLY ONCE. I'D BETTER GATHER SOME HUMANS WHO WILL BE SACRIFICED TO CAST THE SPELL.
OH!
SEND ME. I'LL BRING THEM TO YOU!
WHAT, SO YOU CAN EAT THEM UP AND BRING ME DEAD BODIES? I NEED THEM ALIVE, LINGTSE.
I'LL GO INSTEAD.
HMPH!

콰광
YIKES!
HEY, NOT BAD! WHAT WAS THAT?
THAT WAS THE SAGES' OPENING SHOT, MY DEARS...

NOW, MY BELOVED DISCIPLES...
SHOW THEM WHAT DEMONS ARE CAPABLE OF!
YES SIR!
YUAE, WAKE UP YOUR LITTLE PET AND HELP BLOCK THE ADVANCE OF THOSE DREADNOUGHTS AND DIVINE SOLDIERS.
GOT IT!
KUCHA, WAKE UP AND HELP ME!
GRRRR!!!

PAORIN, SET UP YOUR FORMATION HERE.
YES, MASTER.
CHUN AND LINGTSE, FOLLOW ME.

I WONDER WHAT PAORIN IS DOING?

촤악
쿠우...

GRRRR...
WHO DARES CALL ME FORTH TO THE HUMAN REALM WITH THE BLOOD OF AN ENVOY?
LONG TIME NO SEE, SONG EMPEROR.
PAORIN...I SHOULD HAVE KNOWN.
YOU HAVE DEFILED THE BLOOD OF YOUR ANCESTORS WHO SERVED ME LOYALLY AS ENVOYS. WHAT IS IT THAT YOU DESIRE NOW?

I'LL SACRIFICE THE SOULS OF 200,000 IF YOU ACTIVATE THE DEMON GATE TO HADES SPELL FOR TWO HOURS.
200,000... THAT IS AN ACCEPTABLE SACRIFICE. BUT WHERE ARE THE SOULS?
THEY ARE EVERY MAN, WOMAN AND CHILD YOU SEE DOWN HERE...
...EXCEPT FOR THOSE IN THAT TOWER.

IS THAT WHAT I THINK IT IS?

THE SONG EMPEROR!

BUT WHAT GOOD WOULD HE DO IN THIS FIGHT?

WEAK HUMANS, YOUR SOULS BELONG TO ME NOW.

HELP!

SAVE US!

AAAH!

NO!

I COLLECT YOUR SOULS AND COMMAND THE WIND OF DESTRUCTION TO SWEEP OVER THIS LAND!
HAHAHAH

!!
쿠쿠쿠쿵
HE'S TRANSFORMING THE CITY WITH DEMON ENERGY! WE MUST STOP HIM!
MY FELLOW SAGES, IF HE SUCCEEDS WE WILL BE IN TROUBLE!

HA HA HA, LORD HEIAN WORRIES TOO MUCH.
WE HAVE HIS SAGES, THE DREADNOUGHTS, AND MY MEN...
THE DEMONS WILL BE NO MATCH FOR US!
......

FEEL MY BLADE, TAORUN!
NOT BAD, SHOUREN. YOUR SWORDSMANSHIP HAS IMPROVED OVER THE YEARS.
GRR.
캉
캉
캉
YAH!

流派東方

UGH!
NICE MOVE...
I SEE THAT YOU'VE WORKED VERY HARD, SWORD SAGE.
WHA --?!
BUT YOU STILL HAVE THE BAD HABIT OF NOT LOOKING AROUND YOU WHEN YOU FIGHT.

I SUMMON THEE TO RISE, AND THE EARTH TO TURN INTO HELL!
RISE!

SILENCE...
THEY BLUFF, LORD HEIAN. THEIR SPELL WILL AMOUNT TO NOTHING!
COMMANDERS, GET READY TO SEND OUT THE DIVINE SOLDIERS!
......
YES, GENERAL!
LIFT YOUR SPEARS, MEN!

HUH?!
NO! WE'RE UNDER ATTACK!
MEN, DISEMBARK AND LAUNCH AN ALL-OUT ATTACK!

HA HA...
THIS SPELL IS CALLED THE IRON HAMMER, YUAE. IT POUNDS AWAY AT THE ENEMY UNTIL EVERYTHING HAS BEEN PULVERIZED.
HMM?
후후후...

COMBINED WITH THE DEMON GATE SPELL, IN LESS THAN TWO HOURS THERE WILL BE NOTHING LEFT OF THIS CITY EXCEPT FOR A HELLISH WASTELAND. AND SINCE THE DEMON SPELL DOES NOT HAVE ANY EFFECT ON US, WE'LL BE ABLE TO FIGHT WITHOUT A PROBLEM.
할짝
OKAY, BUT WHAT ABOUT KUCHA?
I DON'T KNOW ABOUT YOUR PET.
BUT DOES IT EVEN MATTER? WE CAN FIND SOME WAY TO RECONSTRUCT HIS BODY, I'M SURE.

탁

I'LL NEVER LET THAT HAPPEN TO KUCHA!

HO!
THIS DEMON HAS BLOCKED MY SAGE HAMMER!
HEE HEE! MY TURN!
I'LL SHOW YOU WHAT LITTLE LINGTSE CAN DO!
ACK!

OOH, GIRL FIGHT!

Spear of Blazing Petals!

THERE IS NO PLACE FOR THE DEMON RACE IN THIS REALM.

HEE...
YOU REALLY THINK YOU CAN HURT ME WITH THOSE?
BLOOM MY FLOWERS, AND BLAZE A TRAIL ACROSS THE SKY!

Blazing petals bloom into fire!
HEE HEE, STOP IT! THIS TICKLES!
Shrapnel Blossom!
Blazing petals bloom into fire!

UGH!

HEY SAGE, THANKS FOR THE FLOWERS! NOW I HAVE A DELIVERY FOR YOU!

SIS!
SHUPA, I'M OKAY. GO HELP LADY SOHWA. HURRY!
AAGH!
FORGIVE ME, SAGE HYUNGWAN!
SOME-THING IS INTERFERING WITH OUR DIVINE POWERS...
IF WE COULD USE THEM, WE'D BE FARING MUCH BETTER IN THIS FIGHT!

SHE TAKES MY BREATH AWAY!
THAT DEMON CHUN, HOW BEAUTIFUL SHE IS!
...

I WAS, UH, SIMPLY EXPRESSING MY WONDER AT HER MARVELOUS SKILLS, EVEN IF SHE IS AN ENEMY OF OURS.
I WASN'T JOKING, SAGE KOCHUN.
THIS IS NO TIME TO BE JOKING, LADY RYUHWA!
화악
EITHER WAY...
크아!!
...HELP US GET HER!
ACH!

KOCHUN, WE HAVE TO STOP THAT DEMON!
BEFORE IT'S TOO LATE!
I KNOW, SAGE CHUNGYEE!
EVERY TIME HER SWORD FLASHES, SEVERAL OF OUR SOLDIERS FALL UNDER ITS BLADE!

캉
카아아
캉
카캉

I'M IMPRESSED AT YOUR IMPROVEMENT, MY STUDENT, BUT YOU'LL HAVE TO TRAIN ANOTHER HUNDRED YEARS BEFORE YOU HAVE ANY CHANCE OF SLAYING ME.

DAMN IT! I CAN'T GET CLOSE ENOUGH TO TAORUN TO DO ANY DAMAGE!

YOU DARE CALL YOURSELF MY TEACHER?

SHOUREN, YOU DISAPPOINT ME.
IF YOU THINK I HAVE TAUGHT YOU NOTHING...
...THEN LET ME SHOW YOU THIS...
OBSERVE, THE ULTIMATE MANIFESTATION OF VEILED SWORDCRAFT...
!!

Divine Demon Sword Strike!

OPEN YOUR EYES AND LOOK, MY STUDENT.
THIS IS THE DIVINE DEMON SWORD STRIKE. IT DOESN'T GET ANY BETTER THAN THIS.

Divine Demon Sword Strike!

Take flight!

ANOTHER LESSON: FELL THE ENEMY GENERAL AND HIS TROOPS WILL BE CRUSHED ALL THE FASTER.

OH, NO!
HUCK...
GENERAL!
I... I WON'T GO DOWN LIKE THIS, LORD HEIAN!
DREAD-NOUGHTS... SELF-DESTRUCT!

WHAT ?!
GENERAL, WHAT ARE YOU DOING?! YOU'LL KILL EVERYONE!!!
GENERAL LEE!
I GAVE THE ORDER... SELF-DESTRUCT!!
KAF!!

?!

EVERYONE, PROTECT YOURSELVES!

YUAE, LINGTSE, CHUN! TAKE SHELTER IN THE TOWER!
HURRY!
PAORIN!
ACTIVATE A PROTECTIVE SHIELD AROUND THE CITY!
YES!

YIKES!
...
...AND THAT'S WHAT HAPPENED.
SO THE EXPLOSION AND THE EARTHQUAKE WERE ALL BECAUSE OF YOU, I SEE.
WHAT DO YOU MEAN BECAUSE OF ME?
IF THOSE DREADNOUGHTS HADN'T SELF-DESTRUCTED, NONE OF THIS WOULD HAVE HAPPENED!

AND IF POOR KUCHA HADN'T PROTECTED ME...

SNIFF

SNIFF

GOOD GRIEF. WHAT ARE YOU SNIFFLING ABOUT AGAIN?

WAAA...

흑

IN SAVING ME, KUCHA GOT REALLY HURT ...

흑

KUCHA, YOU MEAN THE STONE MONSTER?

SNIFFLE... HE'S NOT A MONSTER!

HE'S A LIFE FORM THAT OUR TRIBE CREATED FROM DEAD MATTER.
KUCHA WAS MY FRIEND WHEN MY TRIBE WAS IN THE HEAVENLY REALM.
HE IS SMALL, BUT HE CAN DRAW ON ALL THAT SURROUNDS HIM TO BECOME BIGGER.
?
AND HE'S STRONG, TOO!
OKAY, OKAY! I GET THAT YOU LIKE YOUR PET!
WHAT'S MORE IMPORTANT...

...IS WHAT I'M GOING TO DO WITH YOU.
EH?
움찔
I DON'T LIKE DEMONS.
....
....

......

OHHH, NOOO...
SPARE ME, PLEASE!
HEY, NOT THE CRYING AGAIN!
GEEZ, FINE! I WON'T KILL YOU!
BUT YOU'RE GOING TO HAVE TO ANSWER EVERY QUESTION I ASK YOU.
UNDER-STOOD?

I SPARED YOUR LIFE, BUT YOU DO MY BIDDING FROM NOW ON!
GULP!
WHA?
HEH!

휘이이이잉

...
I DON'T BELIEVE YOU, SHIYAN!
YOU MUST. SHYAO'S REAL IDENTITY IS RANA, THE LADY SOHWA, ONE OF THE EIGHT GREAT SAGES.

THOUGH YOU KNEW HER AS SHYAO LIN WHEN SHE MASQUERADED AS A HUMAN, SHE WAS BORN A SAGE... WHICH MEANS THAT HER ENERGY IS PARTICULARLY CLEAN AND POWERFUL.
IF YOU ABSORB IT, YOUR STRENGTH WILL INCREASE GREATLY.
SHUT UP!
IF I EVER HEAR YOU SUGGEST THAT AGAIN...
...I'LL SLIT YOUR THROAT!

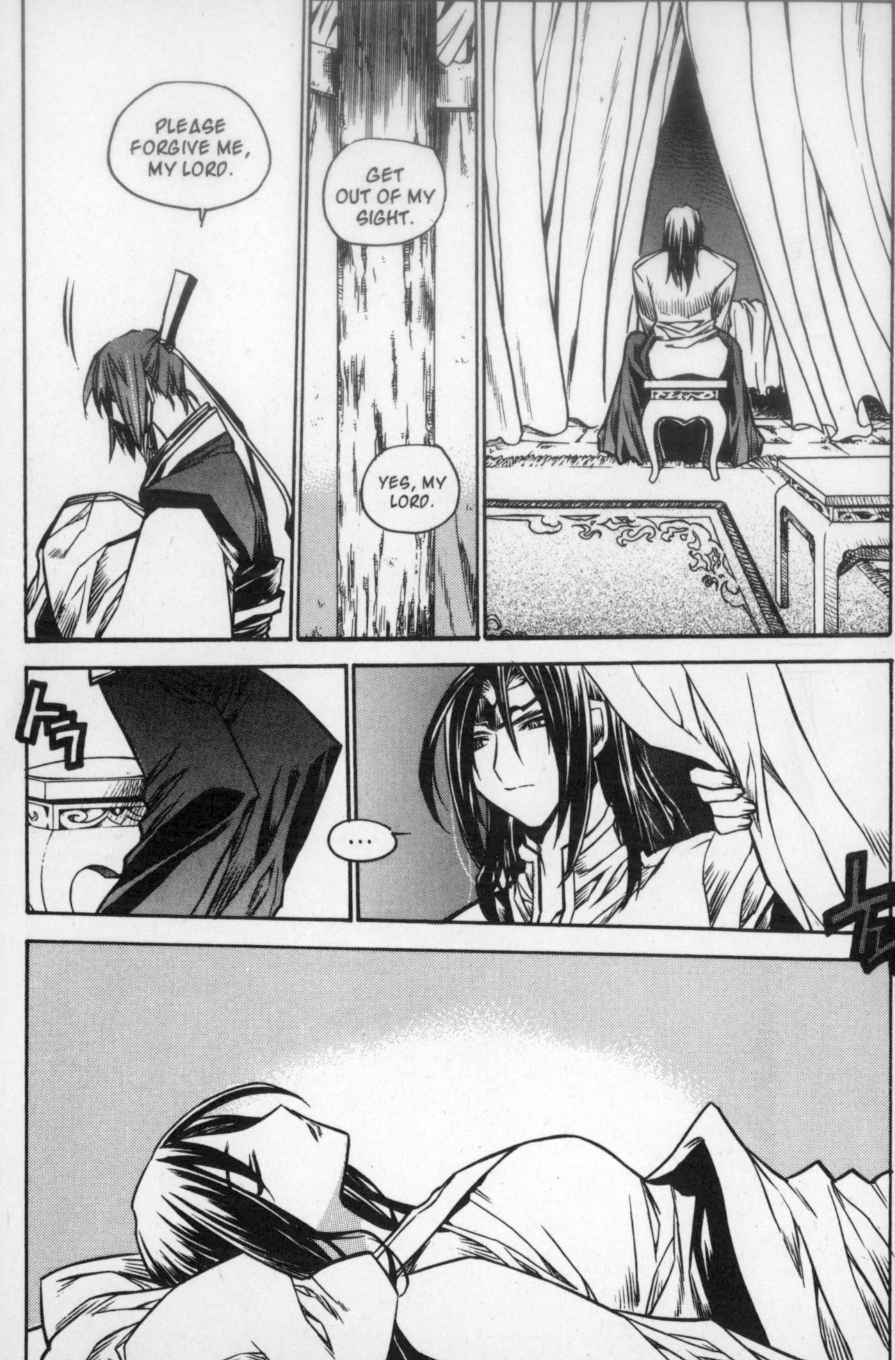
PLEASE FORGIVE ME, MY LORD.
GET OUT OF MY SIGHT.
YES, MY LORD.
...

MY DEAR SHYAO, IT DOESN'T MATTER TO ME WHO YOU REALLY ARE...

I'M JUST GLAD I FOUND YOU AGAIN, AT LAST.

HERE YOU ARE, LYING IN MY BED.

AND I SWEAR I'LL DO ANYTHING...

...TO MAKE YOU MINE!

REST...
I WON'T LET ANYONE COME NEAR YOU.

저벅
저벅
I NEED TO MAKE SURE YOU WILL BE SAFE...
AND IF ANYONE DARES THREATEN YOU, I'LL KILL THEM!

I WILL NEED MORE POWER.

SHIYAN!
YOUR MAJESTY?
READY THE MEN. I WANT TO TAKE 50,000 WITH ME.
WHILE I'M GONE, I EXPECT YOU TO OVERSEE LADY SHYAO'S TREATMENT.

BUT OF COURSE.

WHY MUST I BE TREATED THIS WAY?

UM...EXCUSE ME...

BECAUSE YOU'RE A HOSTAGE!

I'M NOT A DOG. WHY PUT A CHAIN AROUND MY NECK?

STILL...

BE QUIET! OTHERWISE, I'LL PUT CHAINS AROUND YOUR WRISTS AND ANKLES, TOO!

PRISONERS ARE SUPPOSED TO BE TREATED THIS WAY!

AND SINCE YOU'RE A GIRL, I'M EVEN TRYING TO GO EASY ON YOU!

AHH!

NOW, WHERE IS THAT OLD HAG, LAOBI? THE SUN IS ALMOST DOWN!

SOB!

HEY YOU TWO, SHHH!!!

IF SHE HEARD YOU GUYS JOKING LIKE THAT, ALL HELL WOULD BREAK LOOSE!

HA, I KNOW! MAYBE DR. LAOBI'S AGE SUDDENLY CAUGHT UP WITH HER AND SHE BROKE HER LEG OR SOMETHING! HA HA HA!

잉잉

잉잉...

SHE'S A SCARY, SCARY WOMAN.
DON'T CALL HER AN "OLD HAG" OR THE "RED WITCH," OKAY?
...
HMM?
IS SHE REALLY THAT SCARY?
SHE'S TERRIFYING!
PEOPLE HAVE BEEN SCARED OF HER FOR OVER A HUNDRED YEARS!
나닥
헤에
HER REPUTATION HAS SPREAD GENERATION AFTER GENERATION...

SEE, SHE LOOKS REALLY YOUNG...

...BUT SHE'S REALLY A CRAGGY OLD WITCH!

HA HA HA

YUCK!

!

WHAT WAS THAT, LOUEN?

YOU SHOULDN'T...

...TALK ABOUT A WOMAN'S AGE.

AFTER ALL, NOT MINDING YOUR MANNERS CAN SOMETIMES GET YOU KILLED!

......
허걱

GRR...

UM, IT'S NOT WHAT YOU THINK.

I WAS JUST REPEATING...
...WHAT MAO AND REY SAID FIRST!
I DIDN'T SAY ANYTHING, DON'T POINT AT ME!

THAT'S RIGHT!
REY AND I WERE JUST WAITING AROUND. LOUEN AND THE DEMON GIRL WERE THE ONES WHO WERE TALKING ABOUT YOU...
HEY, WHAT?!
휘잉
IS THAT SO?
저벅
GULP!
저벅
IS THAT TRUE, DEMON?
UM...
UM...
UM...

I...

I...WAS JUST...

...LISTENING TO WHAT *HE* WAS SAYING, THAT'S ALL!

!!

...

AARRGH!

I CAN'T BELIEVE YOU GUYS!

WHAT ?!

OH, NOOOO!!!

REY, WHY DO WE HAVE TO SET OUT SO EARLY?
I STAYED UP ALL NIGHT. I'M EXHAUSTED!
OH, MY SHOULDER ...
WE'RE ALMOST THERE. WE CAN GET TO THE GREAT AZURE PAVILION IN THREE DAYS IF WE HURRY.
UMM, DR. LAOBI?
IS LOUEN GOING TO BE ALL RIGHT?
JUST YOU LEAVE HIM ALONE, MAO.
I'M MAKING HIM SPEND ALL DAY WITH THOSE NEEDLES IN HIS FACE.
오호호호~

THREE DAYS...

...AND THEN I'LL GET TO SEE SHYAO AGAIN!

OF COURSE, I FEEL SORRY FOR MYSELF, TOO...

WE'LL BE IN FINE SHAPE IF WE CAN GET OUT OF THIS VALLEY TODAY.
웅성
웅성
EH?
WHAT ARE ALL THOSE PEOPLE DOING HERE?
酒幕
HELLO STRANGERS. ARE YOU ON YOUR WAY TO THE GREAT AZURE PAVILION?
YES.
WE ARE!

THE EARTHQUAKE A FEW DAYS AGO MADE THE ROAD AHEAD IMPASSABLE.
YOU'LL PROBABLY HAVE TO STAY HERE AT MY INN FOR AT LEAST TWO, THREE DAYS.
BUT WHO KNOWS, IT MIGHT TAKE AS LONG AS A MONTH TO RESTORE THE ROAD.
A MONTH ?!
THAT CAN'T BE!
IF YOU DON'T BELIEVE ME, ASK THOSE GUYS OVER THERE. THEY JUST WENT TO SEE IT FOR THEMSELVES.
THIS STINKS!
THE ROAD IS COMPLETELY BLOCKED!
GRRR...
DOES THIS MEAN WE HAVE TO GO AROUND?
!

KOUCHIEN, LOOK! REY YAN, IS THAT YOU?!
CHEN KAIHU? KOU-CHIEN?
DON'T YOU MEAN **MASTER** KAIHU, REY? YOUR MANNERS ARE STILL DESPICABLE!
DODGING MY BLOWS, EH? I SEE YOU'VE BEEN PRACTICING YOUR SKILLS!
휘익
WOWSA!
WHO IS **THIS** MISERABLE WRETCH?!

WE MEET AGAIN, REY YAN.
YES.

*Editor's Note: see Vol. 8 for one heckuva fight!

키잉

EASY DOES IT, REY.
!

에...
—.—

I GUESS WE WILL HAVE TO FINISH OUR FIGHT HERE, SAGE.

...
AS A MATTER OF FACT, I AM.

WHAT, ARE YOU SWEET ON HER OR SOME-THING?

YOU PROTECT HER, KOU-CHIEN?

WHAT?! HE DOESN'T KNOW SAGE RYUHWA IS REALLY A MAN??!!
EVEN JUNIOR SAGES KNOW THAT ONE!
퍼—헉

OH... REALLY?
SPEECHLESS!
TH-THANKS...
UMM...ARE YOU GUYS...DATING OR SOMETHING? UM, WELL..IF YOU ARE...
...I GUESS I CAN LET OUR DIFFERENCES SLIDE FOR NOW...
IS THE ROAD REALLY BLOCKED?
YEAH, IT'S IMPAS-SABLE.
I TRIED FORCING MY WAY THROUGH, BUT I THINK THAT WOULD ONLY MAKE IT WORSE.
HEE HEE!
?
WOULD YOU SHOW US?
HMM.

WOW, IT'S A HUGE MESS!

MAO

I TOLD YOU. WE CAN'T EVEN CLIMB OVER IT.

KOUCHIEN

IT DOESN'T LOOK THAT BAD. ALL WE NEED IS A SMALL PATH THROUGH, RIGHT?

LET ME TRY THIS!

BE CAREFUL!

Moonbeams...

...Slice Through the Night Air!

AND FOR THE FINISHING TOUCH...

OHO! HE **HAS** GOTTEN BETTER!

YAA!

INDEED, HE'S IMPROVED BY LEAPS AND BOUNDS!

MARVELOUS!

THAT WAS NOTHING, REALLY. IT HARDLY TOOK ANY EFFORT AT ALL.

GREAT! NOW I'LL BE ABLE TO ACCOMPANY SHUANGPANG TO THE GREAT AZURE PAVILION!

YOU'RE GOING THERE, TOO?

YES. TO HEAL HER INJURIES, WE NEED TO GET TO THE PAVILION.

OH, I SEE.

COME ON. IF WE HURRY, WE CAN MAKE IT THERE BY NIGHTFALL!

HUH?

YIKES... WHAT IS THAT?!

LAND-SLIDE!
—!
LOOK OUT!
RUN! HURRY!
YIKES!
WHOA!
LET'S GET OUT OF HERE!
SAVE US!
STUPID REY!
GRRRR!
.....

Chapter 62: Mother?!

REY, YOU IDIOT!
THANKS TO YOU, NOW THERE'S NO ROAD AT ALL!
헉
헉
헉
헉
헉
헉
헉
HUFF HUFF HUFF HUFF
....
크윽
WE HAVE NO CHOICE. WE'LL HAVE TO HEAD TOWARD THE VALLEY...
LET'S JUST HOPE THAT WAY ISN'T BLOCKED, TOO.
OKAY, LET'S GO.
WE'LL HAVE TO HURRY IF WE WANT TO SLEEP SOMEWHERE WARM TONIGHT.
SIGH...
헉

OH, NO! THIS PATH IS BLOCKED, TOO!

GREAT. PERFECT. NOW WE HAVE A ROUGH ROAD AHEAD, THANKS TO THE IDIOT AMONG US.

...

WELL, WE'LL HAVE TO CAMP OUT HERE TONIGHT.

TOMORROW WE'LL FIND A WAY AROUND THE MOUNTAIN. IT WILL PROBABLY SET US BACK A FEW DAYS.

REY, YOU HAVE GROWN SINCE WE LAST SAW EACH OTHER.

YOUR EXECUTION OF THE MOONBEAM TECHNIQUE IS MUCH SHARPER. WOULD YOU LIKE TO LEARN THE REST OF THE TECHNIQUES?

흘흘...

YEAH, WHY NOT?

I COULD USE SOME MORE WEAPONS. SHOW ME WHAT YOU'VE GOT, OLD MAN.

"OLD MAN"?!

COME ON, HOW AM I SUPPOSED TO ADDRESS YOU?
HMPH!
HOW ABOUT "OH, MAGNIFICENT WARRIOR," OR "GREAT ONE," OR EVEN JUST "MASTER"?
HMM...
ALL OF THOSE WOULD DO.

HA! SUCH AN EGO!

FINE.
I THINK I'LL JUST CALL YOU "GRAMPS." I NEVER KNEW MY GRANDPA...

GRAMPS? THAT'S THE SAME AS "OLD MAN"!
I'M NOT THAT OLD!
NOT OLD? BOY, YOU ARE DELUDED.

YOU'RE ONE TO TALK OF DELUSION, REY YAN.

MASTER.
STRANGE... I FEEL SUCH A CHILL IN HER PRESENCE!

YOU WANT SOMETHING, DOCTOR?
NO, NOTHING.
BUT I **WAS** HOPING YOU MIGHT FORMALLY INTRODUCE ME TO OUR NEW COMPANIONS.

SURE. THIS LITTLE OLD MAN IS--
빠악

MASTER CHEN KAIHU AT YOUR SERVICE, MADAM.

OWW...!

I AM KOUCHIEN.

HM. I'VE HEARD OF YOU TWO BEFORE. YOUR REPUTATIONS AS FIGHTERS PRECEDE YOU.

MY NAME IS CHEN LAOBI, DOCTOR EXTRA-ORDINAIRE.

YOU SEE SOMETHING IN MY FACE, MASTER KAIHU? ARE YOU SURE THAT'S IT?

HA HA HA...

저벅

움찔

NO...

IT CAN'T BE...

OR COULD IT, MASTER? COULD IT BE THAT YOU'VE FOUND OUT WHO I AM...

...MY DARLING AHMING?

?

...

...MOTHER ?!

MOTHER?!
YOU REMEMBER!
MY SON! ♡

AHMING, YOU LEFT HOME WHEN YOU WERE TWENTY, AND I THOUGHT I WOULD NEVER SEE YOU AGAIN!
I CAN'T BELIEVE I'VE FOUND YOU!
PLEASE, REY AND KOUCHIEN, GIVE US SOME FAMILY TIME ALONE.

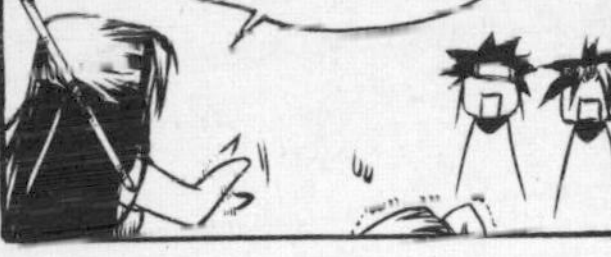
MAN, I'M NOT SURE I'D LIKE HER AS A MOM...
...
MY LITTLE AHMING, YOU'VE GOTTEN SO OLD!
HOW HAVE YOU BEEN ALL THESE YEARS? AND, MORE IMPORTANTLY, HOW IS THE TOME OF MARTIAL ARTS SECRETS YOU STOLE WHEN YOU LEFT HOME? I HOPE YOU'VE KEPT IT SAFE...
YES, YES...EVEN IF IT TAKES ALL NIGHT, WE HAVE A *LOT* OF CATCHING UP TO DO, MUA HA HA HA...

I DON'T UNDERSTAND WHAT'S GOING ON.
HOW COULD MASTER KAIHU HAVE SUCH A YOUNG MOTHER?

DR. LAOBI LOOKS YOUNG, BUT SHE'S REALLY ISN'T. SHE SAYS SHE'S 150 YEARS OLD. I GUESS SHE'S LEARNED A THING OR TWO ABOUT LOOKING YOUNG FROM ALL HER AWFUL EXPERIMENTS ON PEOPLE. STILL, AS FOR HER BEING MASTER KAIHU'S MOTHER, I'M JUST AS SHOCKED AS YOU ARE.

WOW.
THE WHOLE THING'S GIVING ME A HEADACHE.
THEY AREN'T THE ONLY ODD COUPLE. ARE YOU AND SAGE RYUHWA REALLY AN ITEM?

...?

하아

UGH, NOW *THAT'S* A LONG STORY!

I'VE BEEN AGONIZING OVER IT.

A WHILE BACK, I RAN INTO HER AGAIN.

WHEN I SAW HER, I WANTED TO KILL HER...

SHUANGPANG! WHAT THE HELL IS *HE* DOING HERE?

UGH.
JUST WHEN I THOUGHT I COULD FORGET ABOUT THAT DISGUSTING EPISODE AT THE BATHING SPRINGS...
MMNN...
I SHOULD KILL HIM!
GRRR... HOW DARE HE MAKE A FOOL OUT OF ME!
AH...
WHERE AM I?
OH!

TAKE THAT, YOU IMPOSTOR!
WAIT! KOUCHIEN ?!
YOU REMEMBER ME?
YES, OF COURSE! WE MET AT THE GREAT AZURE PAVILION!
WHY ARE YOU ATTACKING ME?!

WHY AM I ATTACKING YOU?

EH?

SHUANGPANG, FROM THE MOMENT I SAW YOU, I FELL IN LOVE WITH YOU!

YOU WENT AROUND IN DRAG, CONFUSING EVERYONE, AND INSULTED MY HONOR!

AND THEN, **YOU TURNED OUT TO BE A MAN!!!**

STILL...
YOU'RE STILL A MAN PHYSICALLY, NO?
YES, FOR NOW... BUT IF MY SAGELY POWERS INCREASE, I WILL BE ABLE TO CHANGE MY BODY AT WILL!
AND IF FOR SOME REASON THAT BECOMES IMPOSSIBLE, I DON'T CARE IF I HAVE TO GIVE UP BEING A SAGE...I'LL GO BACK TO BEING A PLAIN HUMAN WOMAN!

RE... REALLY?
I'M SO CONFUSED... SO SHOULD I BE THINKING OF HER AS A WOMAN?

ACH...
COUGH
COUGH
WHOA...
...ARE YOU OKAY?

MY WOUNDS... THEY'RE DEEP.
THE GREAT AZURE PAVILION... I MUST GET BACK. I NEED HELP...
I SHOULDN'T HAVE ATTACKED YOU. I'VE MADE YOUR WOUNDS WORSE. LET ME ESCORT YOU TO THE PAVILION.
...
YOU'LL DO THAT FOR ME? I DON'T THINK I CAN MAKE IT ALONE...
YOU CAN DEPEND ON ME!
HEH...
AND EVER SINCE THEN, LADY RYUHWA AND I HAVE BEEN CLOSE. SO YEAH, I GUESS WE'RE SEEING EACH OTHER.
WHAT?
OH MY GOD!
SHUANGPANG IS STILL A MAN!

To be continued in Chronicles of the Cursed Sword Vol. 16.

NEXT VOLUME

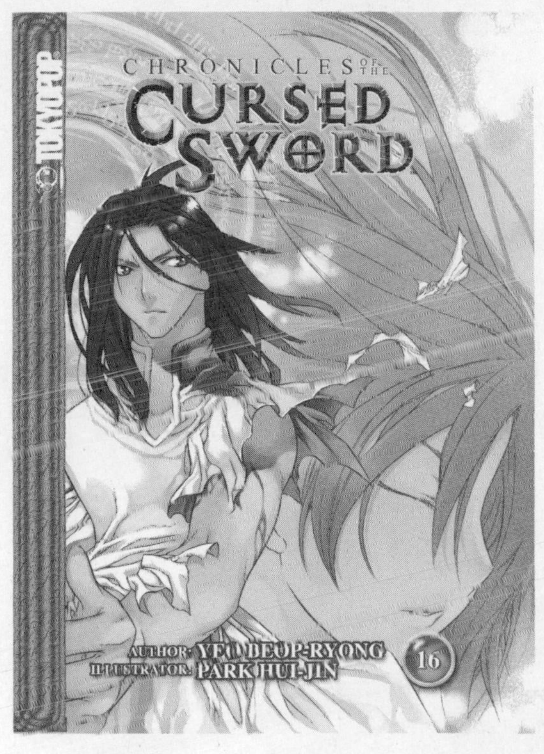

Jaryoon continues to cut a bloody swath through the countryside, killing friend and foe alike, on his way to the Great Indigo Pavillion. Meanwhile, Rey and company enter a territory called "Sohueng County," where they are confronted by one of Jaryoon's underlings. His name is General Gantai, and he is determined to make a name for himself...by killing Rey!

LIFE

BY KEIKO SUENOBU

Ordinary high school teenagers...
Except that they're not.

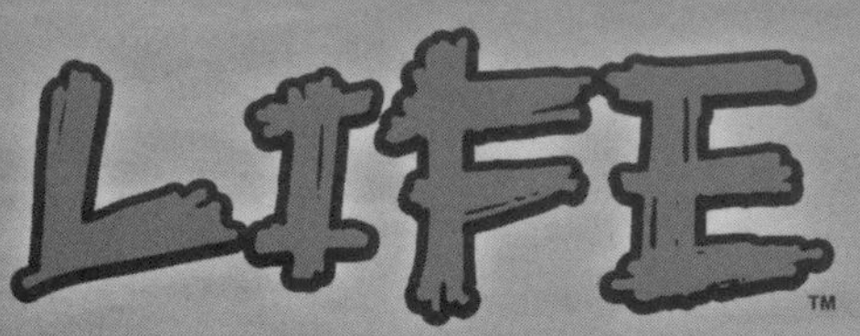

READ THE ENTIRE FIRST CHAPTER ONLINE FOR FREE:

Ayumu struggles with her studies, and the all-important high school entrance exams are approaching. Fortunately, she has help from her best bud Shii-chan, who is at the top of the class. But when the test results come back, the friends are surprised: Ayumu surpasses Shii-chan's scores and gets into the school of her choice—without Shii-chan! Losing her friend is so painful for Ayumu that she starts cutting herself to ease her sorrow. Finally, Ayumu seeks comfort in a new friend, Manami. But will Manami prove to be the friend that Ayumu truly needs? Or will Ayumu continue down a dark path?

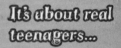

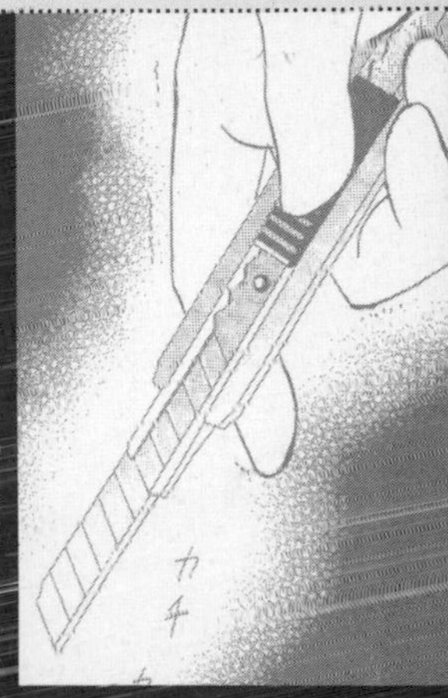

It's about real teenagers...

It's about real high school...

It's about real life.

WWW.TOKYOPOP.COM/LIFE

that I'm not like other people...

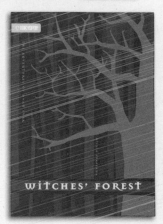